THE FIRE OF
CHRIST'S LOVE

MEDITATIONS ON THE CROSS

THE FIRE OF CHRIST'S LOVE

MEDITATIONS ON THE CROSS

RANIERO CANTALAMESSA, OFM CAP

the WORD among us® Press

Published by The Word Among Us Press
7115 Guilford Drive, Suite 100
Frederick, Maryland 21704
www.wau.org

17 16 15 14 13 1 2 3 4 5

ISBN: 978-1-59325-222-9
eISBN: 978-1-59325-445-8

Cover design by John Hamilton Design

Made and printed in the United States of America

Contents

FOREWORD

When Jesus suffered and died on the cross on that hill called Calvary, on that Friday strangely called "Good," literally, the "lights went out" as even the sun hid in shame, and the earth sobbed with convulsions of sorrow as an earthquake occurred.

Jesus, pure goodness, seemed bullied to death by undiluted evil—

Love, jackbooted by hate;

Mercy incarnate, smothered by revenge;

Life itself, crushed by death.

It seemed we could never smile again.

But then came the Sunday called *Easter!* The sun—S-U-N—came up, and the Son—S-O-N—came out as he rose from the dead. Guess who had the last word? *God!*

Hope, not despair, had the final say;

Faith, not doubt;

Love, not spite;

Light, not an eclipse of the sun;

Life, not the abyss of death.

"He who laughs last, laughs best"—and we believers have never stopped smiling since that resurrection of Jesus from the dead!

So, as the Bible teaches us, if God loves us so much that he didn't even spare his only Son, well, then, "nothing can separate us from the love of God" (cf. Romans 8:35-38), can it?

So, Good Friday did not have the last word—Easter did!

We believe that all is in God's providential hands, and that—the Bible again—All will work out for those who believe" (cf. Romans 8:28).

Lord knows there are plenty of Good Fridays in our lives—but they will not prevail; Easter will. As we Irish claim, "Life is all about loving, living, and laughing, not about hating, dying, and moaning."

That's why a crabby, griping, whining believer is an oxymoron! That's why we say, "*Joy* is the infallible sign of God's presence."

I saw it in Haiti when I went there with Catholic Relief Services right after the devastating earthquake in January 2010. Crying, horror, death, anguish—you bet, in abundance. But still a resilience and a hope in a people clinging onto faith after centuries of oppression and grind.

I see it every time I visit the pediatric oncology department at Sloan-Kettering. Beautiful little innocent children, bald-headed, emaciated by chemo, but they and their folks still radiating an interior trust and calm such that they can smile while I'm choking up.

I see it every time I visit cloistered nuns. Even though they possess nothing of earthly value but the clothes on their back and the prayer books in their hands; even though they live a life of silence, penance, enclosure, and virginity unknown to most of us, they still laugh heartily, and they are the best audience I could ask for in roaring at my corny jokes.

When I was a parish priest, a young man in college once approached me to say that he wanted to become Catholic. When I asked him why, he replied, "Last week I was at the wake of a Catholic man I admired very much, who died suddenly, still young. And his family, while mourning him deeply, could still laugh, as if they knew it would all be okay."

Faith in the cross of Christ and hope in his resurrection does that!

He's hardly a household name, but you should get to know Franciscan Capuchin Fr. Raniero Cantalamessa. Since 1980 he has been the Preacher to the Papal Household and has preached the sermon for Good Friday in St. Peter's Basilica in Rome. Most of us, I know, were unable to be there. But here in this volume are selected "sound bites" of these homilies. As you read this book, perhaps you could imagine yourself sitting in that magnificent basilica, soaking up Fr. Cantalamessa's words. You'd be imagining yourself in good company—Blessed John Paul II and Pope Benedict XVI have heard him preaching these homilies.

The gift that Fr. Cantalamessa brings to us in this book is his ability to shine new perspectives on a topic that we can never fully explore—the cross of Christ. Count on coming away with a new insight, a new way of experiencing "the fire of Christ's love" for you—personally. That's the love that was lifted high on the cross as a sign for the world, a sign that says, "Yes, I love you, beyond all reason, beyond all imagining."

Reading through these selections from Fr. Cantalamessa's sermons reaffirmed my hope in the cross of Christ, because they are filled with important reminders of God's love for each one of us, that he has overcome death and that he is risen! Alleluia!

Even though you may never be in St. Peter's on a Good Friday to hear Fr. Cantalamessa, perhaps you might want to take this book to your own parish church. After praying and meditating on Fr. Cantalamessa's words, take the time to kneel before the crucifix and offer yourself once again to Jesus. It is a fitting response to the One who, through his cross and resurrection, has set us free from sin, given us eternal life, and offers himself to us in the Eucharist at every Mass all over the world each day.

"We adore Thee, O Christ, and we bless Thee! Because by Thy Holy Cross, Thou hast redeemed the world!"

Cardinal Timothy M. Dolan
Archbishop of New York

1. "Were You There When They Crucified My Lord?"

In the New Testament, the kerygma of the passion is always made up of two elements: of a *fact*—he "suffered" and "died"; and of the *reason* for this fact—"for us," "for our sins" (cf. 1 Corinthians 15:3; Romans 4:25). Christ's passion is ultimately unrelated to us unless we enter into it through the narrow door of this "for us," because only he who acknowledges that Christ's passion is his work really understands Christ's passion.

Therefore, my personal sin was also present in Gethsemane, weighing on the heart of Jesus; on the cross, my egoism and my abuse of freedom kept him nailed. If Christ died "for my sins," then—simply by making the phrase active—I killed Jesus of Nazareth! The three thousand whom Peter addressed at Pentecost had not all been present in Pilate's praetorium or on Calvary hammering in the nails, yet he lifted his voice and said to them, "You crucified Jesus of Nazareth!" (cf. Acts 2:23). And by the work of the Holy Spirit, they acknowledged it was true, because it is written, "They were cut to the heart, and said to Peter and the rest of the apostles, 'Brethren, what shall we do?'" (2:37).

"Were you there, were you there, when they crucified my Lord?" says an African-American spiritual full of faith. And it goes on: "Sometimes it causes me to tremble, tremble, tremble." Every time I hear this hymn, I am compelled to think, "Alas, yes, I was also there, I was also there, when they crucified my Lord!"

It is necessary that every man experience an earthquake once in his lifetime and that he experience in his heart something similar to what happened in nature at the moment of Christ's death—the curtain of the Temple was torn in two from top to bottom, the rocks split, and the tombs were opened. It is necessary that a holy fear of God once and for all shatter our hearts, which are so self-confident in spite of everything. Peter the apostle experienced something like this, and he was able to cry out those tremendous words to the multitude because he had first cried them to himself and had "wept bitterly" when Jesus looked at him (Luke 22:62).

In the reading of the passion, we hear these words from John's Gospel: "They shall look on him whom they have pierced" (19:37). May this prophecy be realized in us too; let us look on him whom we have pierced and mourn for him as one mourns for an only child (cf. Zechariah 12:10). If the world is not converted by listening to us preachers of the gospel, let it be converted by seeing us weep and mourn!

2. GOD LOVES YOU!

Why did Jesus die for our sins? The answer was like a flash of sunlight illuminating the faith of the Church: because he loved us! "Christ loved us and gave himself up for us" (Ephesians 5:2); "the Son of God . . . loved me and gave himself for me" (Galatians 2:20); "Christ loved the church and gave himself up for her" (Ephesians 5:25). It is an indisputable primordial truth pervading everything, and it applies both to the Church as a whole and to every individual. St. John the Evangelist, the last to write his gospel, dates this revelation back to Christ when he was on earth: "Greater love has no man than this, that a man lay down his life for his friends. You are my friends" (John 15:13-14).

This answer to the "why" of Christ's passion is really final and allows no further questions. He loved us because he loved us—that's all there is to it! In fact, there is no "why" to God's love; it is a free gift. It is the only love in the world that is truly and totally free, that asks nothing for itself (he already has everything!) but only gives. Or rather, he gives himself. "In this is love, not that we loved God but that he loved us. . . . We love, because he first loved us" (1 John 4:10, 19).

Jesus, then, suffered and died freely, out of love. Not by chance, not from necessity, not because of any obscure forces or historical reasons overwhelming him without his knowledge or against his will. If anyone asserts this, they are nullifying the gospel, removing its soul, because the gospel is nothing other than the good news of God's love in Christ Jesus. Not only the gospel, but the entire Bible is nothing other than the news of God's mysterious, incomprehensible love for people. If the whole of Scripture were to start talking at once, if by some miracle the written words were transformed into speech, that voice would be more powerful than the waves of the sea, and it would cry out: "God loves you!"

3. A Humble and Contrite Heart

Confession of sin when it is sincere and free—what a wonderful thing and how worthy of man it is! It permits God to be himself, as it were, "the God who forgives sin" (cf. Micah 7:18). Siding with God against himself, man induces God to do the same: to side with man against himself and against his own justice. This is obviously out of mercy and not out of need. In fact, God wants to be merciful to the world, but he can't be so if man denies his sin, the very object of God's mercy. The most difficult thing for God to obtain is a "humble and contrite heart." His omnipotence is not sufficient for this; he needs our free response. And that's why it is so precious and touches God's heart.

Thus says the LORD:
"Heaven is my throne
   and the earth is my footstool;
what is the house which you would build for me,
   and what is the place of my rest?. . .
But this is the man to whom I will look,
   he that is humble and contrite in spirit" (Isaiah 66:1, 2).

4. "Father, Forgive Them"

No words can compare with these three: "Father, forgive them" (Luke 23:34). They contain all God's power and holiness; they are indomitable words that no crime or offense can overcome, for they were uttered just when evil was most powerful and at its peak, which it can never reach again. "Death is swallowed up in victory." / "O death, where is thy victory? / O death, where is thy sting?" (1 Corinthians 15:54-55). These words, "Father, forgive them," are like sacramental words. They express the meaning and purpose of the passion—which is the reconciliation of the world with God—and in their expression, they cause it.

This reconciliation began immediately at the cross with those who crucified Christ. I am convinced that these men were saved and that we shall meet them in heaven. They will bear witness for eternity to the extent of the Lord's goodness. Jesus prayed for them with all his power, "Father, forgive them!" and the Father who had always heard his Son's prayer in life (cf. John 11:42) cannot but have heard this prayer of his Son at the moment of death. After the ones who crucified Jesus were forgiven, reconciliation was also extended to the good thief, then the centurion at the foot of the cross, and then the crowd that converted on the day of Pentecost. This procession has gone on swelling and swelling and embraces us who celebrate Christ's death in our own day. In the Book of Isaiah, God says of the suffering servant that he will "make many to be accounted righteous; / . . . because he poured out his soul to death, / and was numbered with the transgressors; / yet he bore the sin of many, / and made intercession for the transgressors" (53:11, 12). Because he took their faults upon himself, saying, "Father, forgive them," he made many to be accounted righteous!

5. Rivers of Living Water

One day, when the Temple of Jerusalem had been destroyed and the people had been exiled to Babylon, the prophet Ezekiel had a vision. He saw before him the rebuilt Temple, and he saw water issuing from below the threshold of the Temple, toward the east. He followed the line of water, and he saw that it was getting deeper and deeper until it was ankle deep, and then knee deep. Then it was up to the loins, and it became a river that he could not pass through. Then he saw upon the bank of the river very many trees, and he heard a voice saying,

> "This water flows toward the eastern region and goes down into the Arabah; and when it enters the stagnant waters of the sea, the water will become fresh. And wherever the river goes every living creature which swarms will live, . . . for this water goes there, that the waters of the sea may become fresh; so everything will live where the river goes." (Ezekiel 47:8-9)

John the Evangelist saw this prophecy fulfilled in Christ's passion. He wrote, "One of the soldiers pierced his side with a spear, and at once there came out blood and water" (John

19:34). The Church sings these words in the liturgy at the beginning of every solemn Mass at Easter time as they now refer to Christ: *Vidi aquam egredientem de templo;* "I saw water issuing from the temple."

Jesus is the temple that man destroyed but that God has rebuilt by raising him from the dead. Jesus had said, "Destroy this temple, and in three days I will raise it up"; and the Evangelist explains that "he spoke of the temple of his body" (John 2:19, 21). On the cross, Christ's body became the new temple, the center of the new worship, the final place of God's glory and presence among men. And from the right side of this new temple, water flows. This, too, like the water seen by the prophet, started as a trickle but grew and grew until it became a big river. In fact, from this trickle of water spiritually comes the water of all the baptistries in the Church. Pope St. Leo the Great had two Latin verses engraved on the Lateran Baptistry, which read: "This is the wellspring that cleansed the whole world—having its source in Christ's wound" (*Fons hic est vitae qui totum diluit orbem— sumens de Christi vulnere principium*). Truly, "rivers of living water" have flowed from the heart of Christ on the cross!

6. PUTTING ON THE HUMILITY OF CHRIST

In the year A.D. 628, Heraclius, emperor of Byzantium, having defeated the Persian King Chosroës, recovered the relics of the Holy Cross that Chosroës had taken away from Jerusalem fourteen years earlier. When he tried to replace the precious relic in the basilica that Constantine had erected on Calvary, a very strange thing happened, which the liturgy commemorates on September 14, the feast of the Exaltation of the Holy Cross. The Office of Readings of that feast day used to tell us that

> Heraclius, completely covered in gold and precious stones, tried to go through the gate that led to Calvary, but he could not move. The more he tried to move ahead, the more he felt nailed to the spot. There was general amazement. Then Zacharias, the bishop, mentioned to the emperor that perhaps his ornamental dress did not suit the humility with which Jesus Christ had crossed the same threshold carrying his cross. The emperor immediately took off his grand clothes and barefoot, in everyday clothes, he moved without difficulty to the spot where the cross was to be replaced.

The rite that the pope performs on Good Friday when, barefoot and without liturgical vestments, he approaches the cross to kiss it, derives from this episode. But there is also a spiritual and symbolic significance that concerns all of us, even those who do not approach the cross barefoot to kiss it. It signifies that we cannot possibly draw near to the crucifix unless we first get rid of our pretensions to greatness, to our rights; in other words, to our pride and vanity. It is simply not possible; we would be invisibly rejected.

And so as we commemorate the Lord's passion, we want to do just two simple things: first, to throw our personal load of pride and that of the world at the foot of the cross; and second, to put on the humility of Christ and with it return home "justified," that is, forgiven, renewed.

7. MARY'S PATH: ONE OF FAITH, NOT VISION

A comparison with Abraham can make the significance of Mary's presence by the cross clearer. It is the angel Gabriel himself at the annunciation who suggested this comparison when he spoke to Mary the same words that had been spoken to Abraham: "With God nothing will be impossible" (Luke 1:37; cf. Genesis 18:14). But it emerges especially from the facts. God promised Abraham that he would have a son even if he was too advanced in years and his wife was barren. And Abraham believed. God announced to Mary that she would bear a son even if she was a virgin. And Mary believed. But then God appeared again to ask Abraham to sacrifice the son he had given him and of whom he had said, "Through Isaac you will have descendants" (cf. Genesis 17:15-21). And Abraham again obeyed. God appeared a second time in Mary's life too, asking her to consent or, rather, to assist in the immolation of her Son, of whom it had been said that he would reign forever and would be great. And Mary obeyed. Abraham climbed Mount Moriah with Isaac, and Mary followed Jesus up Mount Calvary. But much more was asked of Mary than of Abraham. God stopped Abraham at the last minute and restored his son to him, but not with Mary. She had to cross the final threshold of no return, the threshold of death. Her Son was restored to her, but only when he had been taken down from the cross.

As Mary's path was one of faith and not of vision, she hoped that the course of events would change from one minute to the next, that her Son's innocence would be recognized. In vain did she hope in front of Pilate. In vain did she hope along the way to Calvary. She hoped right up to the cross, before the first nail was hammered in, but it was not to be. Had she not been promised that her Son would sit on the throne of David and would reign over the house of Jacob forever (cf. Luke 1:32-33)? Was this cross therefore the throne of David? Mary indeed "in hope believed against hope" (Romans 4:18); she hoped in God even when she saw the last human reason for hope disappear.

Let us now draw the due consequences from this comparison. If for what he did, Abraham deserved to be called "the father of us all" (Romans 4:16) and "our father in faith" (Roman Canon), could we hesitate to call Mary "mother of us all" and "our mother in faith" or "mother of the Church"? God said to Abraham, "Because you have done this, and have not withheld your son, your only son, I will indeed bless you, and I will multiply your descendants. . . . I have made you the father of a multitude of nations" (Genesis 22:16-17; 17:5). And now, more strongly, he says the same thing to Mary, "Because you have done this, and have not withheld your Son, your only son, I will indeed bless you. I have made you the mother of a multitude of nations!"

8. MARY, BLESSED ABOVE ALL WOMEN

There comes a time in life when we need faith and hope like Mary's. It is when God no longer seems to hear us; when he seems to deny himself and his promises; when he makes us face one defeat after another and the powers of darkness seem to triumph on all sides; when, as the psalmist says, he seems to have "in anger shut up his compassion" (Psalm 77:9). When this hour arrives, remember Mary's faith and pray, "Father, I no longer understand you, but I trust you!"

Perhaps God is asking someone to sacrifice, like Abraham, his "Isaac" to him right now—in other words, the person or object, the plan, the foundation or office he holds dear, which God himself entrusted to him one day and to which he has, perhaps, dedicated his life's work. This is the chance God is offering you to show him that he is dearer to you than anything else, dearer than his own gifts or even the work you do for him. God tried Mary on Calvary to see what was in her heart, and in her heart he found the "Yes" and the "Here I am" that she had uttered on the day of the annunciation intact and reinforced. May he now find our hearts ready to say "Yes" and "Here I am."

Mary, as I have said, joined her Son on Calvary in adoring the Father's will. Thus, she realized to perfection her calling within the Church. She is now awaiting us there. It has been said that

"Jesus is in agony to the end of the world. We must not sleep during that time" (Blaise Pascal, *Pensées*, 553). And if Christ is on the cross in agony to the end of time, in a way that is incomprehensible for us but true, where else could Mary be if not close to him, "by the cross" (John 19:25)? It is there that she invites and welcomes generous souls so that they can join her in adoring the holy will of the Father, adoring it even without understanding it. We must not abandon her in this time. Mary knows that this is the greatest, most wonderful, and most worthy thing we can do in life at least once before our death.

It is written that when Judith went back to her people after putting her life at risk for them, the men of the city hurried to meet her and the high priest blessed her, saying, "O daughter, you are blessed by the Most High God above all women on earth; . . . Your hope will never depart from the hearts of men" (Judith 13:18, 19). Today we address the same words to Mary: "Blessed are you above all women! Your hope and courage will never depart from the heart and memory of the Church!"

9. "God, Be Merciful to Me a Sinner!"

It is in my heart that real pride is harbored; pride is the only thing that I can destroy with my own will, as it is the only thing my own will produces.

This is not an easy undertaking! The pearl diver of the South Seas who tries to go deep underwater experiences the tremendous resistance of the water, which vigorously pushes him back up with a force that is equal and contrary to its volume. Without knowing it, he experiences Archimedes' principle. Whoever tries to dive below the calm water of his self-illusion, to humble himself and learn his true self, experiences the even stronger thrust of his own pride, which tends to lift him above himself so that he may emerge and remain on the surface. We, too, are looking for a precious pearl, the most precious in God's eyes. It is called a "humble and contrite heart."

How can we be contrite and humble of heart? Above all, let us seek the help of the Holy Spirit; let us lose the habit of defending ourselves and resisting. Let us look now, if we can, alone before God into the mirror of our conscience: what pride do we have, what vanity and self-complacency, what false humility and hypocrisy, in one circumstance or another, in one attitude or another—maybe, alas, even now at this very moment? How much "I," "I," "I"? "Blush, O dust and ashes, and be ashamed to be proud. God humbles himself and do you exalt yourself?" St. Bernard used to say to himself (*In Praise of the Virgin Mother,* 1, 8). St. Augustine, before him, had said, "Your Lord humble, and you proud? The head humble, and the member proud?" (*Sermons,* 354.9.9; PL 39:1568).

Heaven and earth are filled with the glory of God; only man's heart is an exception, because it is filled with its own glory and not with God's. It is so taken with itself that it uses for its own glory even what was made for God—even God himself! And yet, "What have you that you did not receive?" (1 Corinthians 4:7).

To acquire a contrite and humble heart, we need to be caught out once, like the woman in the gospel who was caught in the act of adultery, who stood there in silence with lowered eyes awaiting her sentence (cf. John 8:3-11). We are thieves caught in the act of stealing God's glory. If now, instead of fleeing elsewhere in thought or allowing ourselves to feel irritated and thinking, "This is a hard saying; who can listen to it?" (John 6:60), let us lower our eyes, strike our breasts, and like the tax collector, let us say from the bottom of our hearts, "God, be merciful to me a sinner!" (Luke 18:13). Then the miracle of a contrite and humble heart will begin to take place in us. And, like the woman, we shall experience the joy of forgiveness instead of condemnation. We shall have a new heart.

10. CHRIST'S CRY OF LOVE

The Evangelists Matthew and Mark describe the death of Christ like this: "Jesus cried again with a loud voice and yielded up his spirit" (Matthew 27:50; cf. Mark 15:37; *kraxas phoné megale* in Greek; *clamans voce magna* in Latin). This cry of Jesus as he died holds a great mystery that we cannot neglect. If it was uttered, it was meant to be heard; if it is written in the gospels, it is part of the gospels. All that had not been said or could not be said in words in the life of Jesus is present in that loud cry. With it, Jesus emptied his heart of all that had filled it in life. It is a cry that pierces the centuries, louder than any human cry of war, of pain, of joy, or of desperation. . . .

The cry of Jesus on the cross was a birth cry. In that moment, a new world was being born. The great dividing wall of sin was being demolished, and reconciliation was taking place. It was therefore a cry of pain and love at the same time. "Having loved his own who were in the world, he loved them to the end" (John 13:1). He loved them with his last breath! We get an idea of the divine power that charged this cry of Christ from what it immediately brought about in those actually listening to it. It is written that when the centurion who stood facing Jesus saw that he had breathed his last, he said, "Truly this man was the Son of God!" (Mark 15:39). He believed.

All we have to do is hear that cry of love and let it move us deep within and change us. Otherwise, Good Friday will pass in vain for us.

11. The Fire of Christ's Love

The fire of Christ's love on the cross has not burnt out; it is not something of the past, of two thousand years ago, of which only the memory lives on. It exists now; it is alive. If it were necessary, Christ would die again for us because the love for which he died continues unchanged. "I am more a friend to you than such and such a one," Christ tells us as once he told the great mathematician and philosopher Blaise Pascal. "I have done for you more than they; they would not have suffered what I have suffered from you, and they would not have died for you as I have done in the time of your infidelities and cruelties, and as I am ready to do, and do, among my elect" (*Pensées*, 553).

Jesus has run out of signs for his love. There is nothing more he can do to show his love, for there is no greater sign than to give one's life. But he has run out of signs for his love, not of love itself. Now his love is entrusted to a special sign, a different one, a sign that is real, a Person: the Holy Spirit. "God's love"—the love we now know—"has been poured into our hearts through the Holy Spirit" (Romans 5:5). It is therefore a living and real love, just as the Holy Spirit is living and real.

Where the other Evangelists say that Jesus "uttered a loud cry and breathed his last" (Mark 15:37; cf. Matthew 27:50),

John says that Jesus "bowed his head and gave up his spirit" (John 19:30). That is, he not only breathed his last, but he gave the Spirit, the Holy Spirit, his Spirit. Now we know what was in the loud cry that Jesus gave us as he was dying. Its mystery has finally been revealed!

12. JESUS CHRIST IS MY LORD

There is a *subjective dimension* in the words "Jesus is Lord!" that depends on the person who is saying them. I have often wondered why the demons in the gospels never once gave Jesus this title. They go as far as saying, "You are the Son of God" or "You are the Holy One of God!" (cf. Luke 4:34, 41; Mark 3:11; 5:7), but they never say, "You are the Lord!" The most plausible reason for this seems that to say, "You are the Son of God" is to simply acknowledge a given fact that does not depend on them and that they cannot change. They know that Jesus is God's Son. But to say, "You are the Lord!" is a different matter. It means to recognize him as such and to submit to his Lordship. If the demons were to do so, they would immediately cease to be what they are and would become angels of light again.

These words divide two worlds. To say, "Jesus is Lord!" means to freely enter his dominion. It is like saying, "Jesus Christ is *my* Lord, the very reason of my existence. I live for him and no longer for myself." St. Paul wrote to the Romans: "None of us lives to himself, and none of us dies to himself. If we live, we live to the Lord, and if we die, we die to the Lord; so then, whether we live or whether we die, we are the Lord's" (14:7-8). The greatest contradiction—that between life and death, ever

present in man—has been overcome. Now the radical contradiction is no longer between living and dying but between living "for the Lord" and living "for oneself." Living for oneself
is the new name for death.

13. Jesus Is Lord of All

L ord" is the divine name that concerns us most directly. God was "God" and "Father" before the existence of the world, the angels, and man, but he was not yet "Lord." He became Lord, *Dominus*, the moment creatures existed over which to exercise his dominion and who freely accepted his dominion. In the Trinity, there are no "lords" as there are no servants, and all three persons are equal. In a certain sense, we make God "Lord"!

God's dominion, rejected by sin, was reestablished by Christ, the new Adam. In Christ, God has become Lord again by an even greater right—that is, not only by creation, but also by redemption. God reigns again from the cross! "For to this end Christ died and lived again, that he might be Lord both of the dead and of the living" (Romans 14:9).

The *objective dimension* of the words "Jesus is Lord" lies in the fact that it makes history present. It is the conclusion of two fundamental events: Jesus died for our sins, and he is risen for our justification; therefore, Jesus is Lord! The events that led up to it are, so to speak, contained in the conclusion and become present and operative in it when we confess it in faith. "If you confess with your lips that Jesus is Lord and believe in your heart that God raised him from the dead, you will be saved" (Romans 10:9).

14. TEARS OF WONDER, TEARS OF GRATITUDE

What will our response be to the revelation of Christ's love? Let us not immediately rush into making proposals and trying to repay it. We would not be able to, and neither is it the most important thing to do today. There is something we must do first of all, the only way to show that we have understood, and that is to feel touched and moved by it. Let us not scorn deep feeling and emotion. When it genuinely comes from the heart, it is the most eloquent and worthy reaction we could possibly have when faced with great love or deep sorrow. A spirit of compassion is a sign that we no longer belong to ourselves. It is opening our intimate selves to another. That is why we are so discreet with it. But we have no right to hide our emotional involvement from the person causing it. It belongs to him, for he caused it, and it is directed to him. Jesus did not hide from the widow of Nain (Luke 7:13) or from the sisters of Lazarus the fact that he was deeply moved; in fact, "Jesus wept" (John 11:35). And are we ashamed to show him that we are deeply moved by his suffering?

Of what use is a spirit of compassion? It is precious because it is like a plow that breaks the hard crust of the soil so that the seed can sink deep into the earth. It is very often the beginning of a true conversion and a new life. Have we ever cried—or, at least, wished to cry—for Christ's passion? There are saints who wept their eyes out over this. "I weep for the passion of my Lord," St. Francis of Assisi used to answer when he was asked the reason for his many tears. It is written, "When they look on him whom they have pierced, they shall mourn for him, as one mourns for an only child" (Zechariah 12:10; cf. John 19:37). And this is not just a prophecy but an invitation, an order, from God.

We have cried enough tears over ourselves—polluted tears, tears of self-pity. It is time to cry other tears—tears of wonder, of joy, of gratitude; tears of compassion even before tears of repentance. It is time to be "born again through water and Spirit" (cf. John 3:5). Often, when I hear the passion being commemorated or I am about to do so myself, Dante's well-known verse comes to my mind, and I repeat it almost angrily to myself: "What do you weep at, if you do not weep at this?" (*Inferno*, XXXIII, 42).

The liturgy of the Church gives us the example. At Easter it is full of feeling. "Father, how wonderful your care for us! How boundless your merciful love! O happy fault which gave us so great a Redeemer!" exclaims the Exultet. Once we have commemorated the cry of Jesus as he died on the cross, let us repeat it: "O happy fault which gave us so great a Redeemer!"

15. God's Painful Embrace

God did not spare his own Son but gave him up for us all" (Romans 8:32). . . . The Church links this text with that of Genesis 22. The text from Genesis talks of Abraham, to whom God says, "Because you have done this, and have not withheld your son, your only son, I will indeed bless you, . . . and by your descendants shall all the nations of the earth bless themselves" (22:16-17, 18).

Abraham, old as he was, walking in silence with his son towards Mount Moriah, was therefore the symbol of another father. He was the symbol of God the Father who accompanied Jesus on his journey to Calvary. When he was leaving the Upper Room, Jesus turned to his disciples and said, "[You] will leave me alone; yet I am not alone, for the Father is with me" (John 16:32).

Who could describe Abraham's feelings as he took his son up Mount Moriah to be sacrificed? The early Church Father Origen said that the most dangerous moment for Abraham was when, along the way, Isaac, in total ignorance of what was happening, turned to his father and said, "My father! . . . Behold, the fire and the wood; but where is the lamb for a burnt offering?" (Genesis 22:7). He had no idea that he was to be the victim. The term "my father," Origen said, was a real temptation for Abraham, and what violence he must have had to do to himself so as not to betray himself and turn back! And when Jesus in Gethsemane said, "Abba, Father, all things are possible to thee; remove this cup from me" (Mark 14:36), who can tell what effect these words had on the Father's heart? Abraham would certainly have preferred a thousand times to die himself instead of killing his son.

Therefore, the heavenly Father and his Son, Jesus, were together in the passion and together on the cross. More than to the wooden arms of the cross, Jesus was nailed to his Father's arms or, as it were, to his will. Just as in eternity it is from the unutterable and joyful embrace between the Father and the Son that the Holy Spirit proceeds—the gift of their mutual love—so now and for all time, it is from that painful embrace of Father and Son on the cross that the Holy Spirit flows—the gift of both of them for us. Jesus "bowed his head and gave up his spirit" (John 19:30).

16. THE REAL JUDGE IS WAITING FOR US

It was appointed for men to die once, and after that comes judgment" (Hebrews 9:27). How human affairs change when seen from this angle, even those in progress today! Every day we hear or read of atrocities aimed at the weak and defenseless, which go unpunished. We witness people involved in organized crime being accused of dreadful crimes and defending themselves with a smile, able to fool the courts and judges and feel safe because proof of their crimes is not forthcoming. It is as if they had solved everything because they are able to get away with it before human judges. But, my poor brethren, you have not managed to get away with anything! The real judgment is still to come. Even if you should end your days in freedom, feared, honored, even having a splendid religious funeral after you have bequeathed large sums of money for works of mercy, you have still not managed to get away with anything. The real Judge is still waiting for you on the other side of the threshold, and he cannot be fooled. God is incorruptible. It is a fearful thing to fall in this state "into the hands of the living God" (10:31).

We know how judgment will take place.

"Then he will say to those at his left hand, 'Depart from me, you cursed, into the eternal fire prepared for the devil and his angels; for I was hungry and you gave me no food, I was thirsty and you gave me no drink, I was a stranger and you did not welcome me, naked and you did not clothe me, sick and in prison and you did not visit me.'" (Matthew 25:41-43)

What will become, then, of those who not only did not give food to the hungry, but even took it from them; of those who not only did not welcome the stranger, but made him a stranger, an exile, a wanderer; of those who not only did not visit the prisoner, but who unjustly imprisoned him, kidnapped, tortured, and killed him?

17. THE WOOD OF THE CROSS

What did "wood" or "tree" represent in the Old Testament? It was the tree of life planted in the Garden of Eden, the tree of the knowledge of good and evil, around which rebellion took place when human beings claimed the right to decide for themselves what is good and what is evil. In the Book of Deuteronomy, the term "wood" or "tree" reappears associated with a curse: "It is written, 'Cursed be every one who hangs on a tree'" (Deuteronomy 21:23, as quoted in Galatians 3:13). But certain passages introduce wood in a positive sense, and these, in the light of what was later fulfilled, are seen as prophecies of the cross. Wood was used to build the ark that saved humanity from the flood (cf. Genesis 6:14); Moses used a wooden staff to divide the waters of the Red Sea (cf. Exodus 14:16); Moses threw a piece of wood into the bitter water at Marah to make it sweet (cf. 15:23-25).

What does the wood of the cross represent in the life of Jesus—in other words, no longer figuratively, but as an actual reality in time and space? It represents the instrument of his condemnation to death, of his total destruction as man, the lowest point of his kenosis. The "tree" (*xulon*), as the cross was often called, was the most infamous death penalty, reserved for slaves guilty of the greatest crimes. Cicero said that even the word was not to be pronounced in the hearing of a Roman citizen. Everything about the penalty was arranged to make it as degrading as possible. First, the condemned man was scourged; then he was loaded with the cross—or at least with its horizontal beam—which he carried to the place of execution. There he was tied naked and then nailed to this instrument of torture, where he died in agony, suffering convulsions and atrocious pain as the weight of his body pulled open his wounds.

"Crucified!" In the apostles' day, no one could hear the word without trembling with fear. And for the Jews, there was the added element of God's curse: "Cursed be every one who hangs on a tree" (Galatians 3:13).

But in the light of the resurrection, what does the cross represent in the age of the Church, according to what the Spirit reveals about it through the apostles? The cross is the place where "the mystery of our religion" (1 Timothy 3:16) is accomplished, where the new Adam says yes to God on behalf of all and for all time. It is where Jesus, the true Moses, divides the true Red Sea with the wood and, by his obedience, transforms the bitter waters of rebellion into the sweet waters of grace and baptism. It is where "Christ redeemed us from the curse of the law, having become a curse for us" (Galatians 3:13). The cross is "the power of God and the wisdom of God" (1 Corinthians 1:24). It is the new tree of life, planted in the heavenly Jerusalem (cf. Revelation 22:2).

What was so decisive about what happened on the cross to justify these statements? What happened was that God finally destroyed sin but without destroying the freedom that produced it. He overcame sin, not by destroying it with his almighty power or driving it out of his kingdom, but by taking it upon himself, in Christ, and suffering the consequences. He overcame evil with good, which is the same as saying that he overcame hatred with love, rebellion with obedience, violence with meekness, falsehood with the truth. "He himself bore our sins in his body on the tree" (1 Peter 2:24). He has freed us for all time.

18. No More Condemnation!

In Franz Kafka's novel *The Trial*, the author tells the story of a man who is placed under arrest while going about his ordinary life and work. No one knows why. He begins the painstaking task of trying to discover the reasons, where the trial would take place, the charges against him, and the procedures. But no one can tell him anything except that there really is a trial going on, and he is the defendant. Then one day they come to take him away for execution. It is the story of humanity struggling even to the point of death to free itself from an obscure sense of guilt that it cannot shake off.

In the course of the story, we learn that there are three possibilities open to the man: he could either be fully acquitted, or apparently acquitted, or the case could be adjourned. But an apparent acquittal or an adjournment would solve nothing—the accused man would just be kept in a state of mortal anxiety for the rest of his life. On the other hand, if he were fully acquitted, all the records of the trial would have to be destroyed. Not only the charges against him but the trial itself and even the sentence would have to be cancelled from the record. Everything would have to be destroyed. But no one knows if there has ever been such a case of full acquittal. There are only rumors, no more than "beautiful legends." Like all of Kafka's works, the novel ends at this point: with something glimpsed in the distance, which you dream about but can never reach.

On Good Friday, we can cry out to the millions of men and women who see themselves represented in that accused man: complete acquittal does exist! It is not a legend, not a lovely dream you can never reach! No. Jesus has "canceled the bond which stood against us with its legal demands; this he set aside, nailing it to the cross" (Colossians 2:14). "There is therefore now no condemnation for those who are in Christ Jesus" (Romans 8:1). No more condemnation! Of any kind! For those who believe in Christ Jesus!

19. Overcoming Death

The Christian faith . . . simply and majestically tells us that death does exist, that it is the biggest of our problems, but that Christ defeated it! A very decisive human event took place, and human death is no longer the same. In faith we are given the incredible news about something that only the coming of God himself on earth could bring about. Death has lost its sting, like a serpent whose poison can only anaesthetize its victim for a short time but cannot kill him. "Death is swallowed up in victory." . . . / "O death, where is thy sting?" (1 Corinthians 15:54, 55).

In the gospel this news about death is proclaimed by a Roman centurion: "And when the centurion, who stood facing him, saw that he thus breathed his last, he said, 'Truly this man was the Son of God!'" (Mark 15:39). This centurion knew all there was to know about combat and combatants, and he immediately understood that the loud cry Jesus uttered when he breathed his last was the cry of a victor and not of one defeated.

How, then, did Jesus overcome death? Not by shunning it, but by accepting it, savoring all its bitterness. He overcame it from within, not from outside. . . .

In Gethsemane, Jesus fully experienced human anguish in the face of death. "He began to be sorrowful and troubled"

(Matthew 26:37), the gospel tells us, and those two words, "sorrowful" and "troubled," suggest the idea of profound bewilderment, a kind of solitary terror, like someone who feels cut off from human society.

Jesus did not face death like someone with an ace up his sleeve to pull out at the right moment. At times during his life, he showed us that he knew he would rise again, but this was a special knowledge that he was not favored with when and as he wished. His cry on the cross, "My God, my God, why hast thou forsaken me?" (Matthew 27:46), shows that this certainty was not available to him, as man, at that moment.

Jesus faced death as we do, like someone who crosses a threshold in the dark and cannot see what is beyond. He was sustained only by his steadfast faith in the Father, which made him exclaim: "Father, into thy hands I commit my spirit!" (Luke 23:46).

20. Recognizing Christ in the Poor

Jesus of Nazareth identified himself with the poor. He who pronounced the words "This is my body" over the bread said the very same words about the poor. He said so when, talking of what had been done or not done for those who are hungry, thirsty, naked, in prison, or strangers, he solemnly declared, "You did it to me" and "You did not do it to me" (cf. Matthew 25:31-46). It is as if he said, "That ragged beggar in need of something to eat, that poor wretch with hands outstretched, was me . . . it was me!"

I remember when the light of this truth exploded in my mind. I was visiting a mission in a Third World country, and with each new scene of misery I witnessed—whether it was a child in rags, his tummy swollen and his face covered with flies; small groups racing after a garbage truck hoping to pick up something from it at the rubbish dump; or someone covered in sores—it was like a voice booming inside me, saying, "This is my body!" It was an overwhelming experience. The poor person, too, is a *vicarius Christi*, one who stands in Christ's place. Not in the sense that whatever a poor person does is done by Christ, but in the sense that what we do to him, we do to Christ: "You did it to me" (Matthew 25:40).

There is a close link between the Eucharist and the poor. In different ways, they are both Christ's body; he is present in both of them. St. John Chrysostom wrote:

Would you honor Christ's body? Then do not permit him to be despised in his members, that is, in the poor who are in need of clothes. Do not honor him here in church clothed in silk, while outside, you neglect him when he is cold and has no clothes. . . . What advantage is it to Christ if the altar is covered with gold vessels while he himself is starving in his poor? First of all, feed those who are hungry and only then, adorn the altar with what remains. (*Hom. in Matth.*, 50, 3–4; PG 58:508–509)

Throughout the centuries, Christ himself has confirmed this strict and realistic interpretation of his words "You did it to me." One day, Martin, at the time both a soldier and catechumen in Roman service in northern Europe, met a poor man who was naked and frozen stiff. As he had only the cloak he was wearing, he cut it in two with his sword and gave one half to the poor man. That night Christ appeared to him wearing that half of his cloak and saying with obvious pride to the angels around him, "Martin, who is still a catechumen, has clothed me with this cloak" (Sulpicius Severus, *Vita Martini*, 3).

The poor man is Christ, still traveling the world unrecognized, somewhat like those times after his resurrection when he appeared in different disguises: as a gardener to Mary, as a pilgrim to the disciples of Emmaus, and as a passerby to the apostles, standing by the lakeside waiting for them to open their eyes. The first of them to recognize him cried out, "It is the Lord!" (John 21:7). If only the same cry of recognition could issue from our lips, even once, at the sight of some poor wretch: "It is the Lord! It is the Lord!"

21. THE ONE TRUE MYSTERY

We have an urgent need to learn to know the true face of the Father again. This is not something that will take years of hard work, like the work that was necessary to remove the patina of grime that obscured the image of the Father in the Sistine Chapel. Here we need only a lamp to be lit , an illumination of the heart, a revelation by the Spirit. For the true face of the Father is there, clearly shown for all time in the Scriptures. One word tells it all: "God is love!" In the New Testament, the word "God," standing alone, always means God the Father. Therefore, God the Father is Love. "God so loved the world that he gave his only Son" (John 3:16) means that *God the Father* so loved the world.

"Why did God make us?" The *Baltimore Catechism* teaches us to answer this question in this way: "to know Him, to love Him, and to serve Him in this world, and to be happy with Him forever in heaven" (No. 1, Qu. 6). A very good answer, but if we look at it carefully, it answers only one aspect of the question: it tells us the *end* or purpose for which we were created (so that *we* could know and serve and love him). It does not answer the question "What was the *cause* of his creating? What prompted God to create us?" To this our answer would not be "so that we could love him," but rather, "because he loved us." Eucharistic

Prayer IV puts it this way: "You . . . have made all that is, so that you might fill your creatures with blessings and bring joy to many of them by the glory of your light."

Here we have the whole difference between the god of philosophers and the God of the gospel. The god of the philosophers is a god who may be loved and who ought to be loved, but who does not love, who cannot love us human beings, and who would disqualify himself if he were to do so. "God," said Aristotle, "moves the world insofar as he *is loved*" (not insofar as *he loves*!). Revelation tells us exactly the opposite: "In this is love, not that we loved God but that he loved us. . . . We love, because he first loved us" (1 John 4:10, 19).

This is the true mystery of Christianity. One of the most widely read of English Christian writers, C.S. Lewis, has written a book, *The Screwtape Letters,* with a most unusual plot. A junior devil is sent to earth to see to the seduction of a decent young man just recently converted. Inexperienced as this tempter is, he keeps in touch with his uncle, Screwtape, a senior devil who writes to him to advise him how to achieve his goal. (Read in the contrary sense, it is a most perceptive work on vices and virtues.) Through the letters, we get a glimpse of hell and an idea of the kind of conversations that take place down there. What irritates the devils intensely, what they simply do not understand and never will be able to understand, is the love that God has for such miserable creatures as humans. People on earth believe that the greatest mysteries are the Trinity and things like that. Fools that humans are, the devils say, they simply do not see that the true mystery, the one utterly inscrutable mystery, is that God should love them. And I believe that the devils, just this once, are right.

22. VICTORY OVER SATAN

The Evangelist St. Luke ends his account of the temptations of Jesus by saying, "The devil left him, to return at the appointed time" (Luke 4:13, JB). Jesus himself tells us what was this "appointed time" when, very shortly before his passion, he says, "Now sentence is being passed on this world; now the prince of this world is to be overthrown" (John 12:31, JB).

All the writers of the New Testament were of one accord in placing this interpretation on Christ's death. Christ, says the Letter to the Hebrews, "by his death . . . could take away all the power of the devil, who had power over death" (Hebrews 2:14, JB).

Victory over Satan is, of course, not the whole or the only meaning of Christ's passion. Its significance is vastly greater, more positive, than that: "Jesus was to die . . . to gather together in unity the scattered children of God" (John 11:51-52, JB). Nevertheless, we do in some way trivialize the passion of Christ if we try to erase this aspect of victory over the devil and see it only as victory over sin and death.

This same struggle continues after Christ, in his body. The Apocalypse says that, defeated by Christ, "the dragon was enraged with the woman and went away to make war on the rest of her children" (Revelation 12:17, JB). For this reason, Peter the apostle advises Christians, "*Be calm but vigilant,* because your enemy the devil is prowling round like a roaring lion looking for someone to eat" (1 Peter 5:8, JB, emphasis added).

This is why the Christian life has always been and will always be something dramatic, an ongoing battle, a battle not only against "human enemies," creatures of flesh and blood (cf. Ephesians 6:12). We see a reflection of this in the Rite of Baptism, where at the very outset, it calls for a drastic choice of sides: "Do you renounce Satan? Do you believe in Christ?"

Are we, then, to think that Christ's death has changed nothing? That all is as it was before? On the contrary! Satan is no longer free to put his power to use for his own purposes. He sets out to do something with a certain aim in mind, and achieves exactly the opposite; quite against his own will, the purposes he actually serves are those of Jesus and his saints. He is "the power that always wills evil but achieves good" (Goethe, *Faust*, Part 1).

23. GOD IS ON OUR SIDE

There is a Latin hymn, as dear as the "Adoro te devote" to Catholic Eucharistic piety: the "Ave Verum." It is not possible to find a better way to bring to light the link between the Eucharist and the cross. Written in the thirteenth century as an accompaniment to the elevation of the host at Mass, it serves us today equally well as our salutation of Christ raised up on the cross. In no more than five short couplets, it brings us such a great load of meaning:

Hail, true Body, truly born
of the Virgin Mary mild.
Truly offered, wracked and torn,
on the Cross for all defiled,
from Whose love-pierced, sacred side
flowed Thy true Blood's saving tide:
be a foretaste sweet to me
in my death's great agony.
O my loving, Gentle One,
Sweetest Jesus, Mary's Son.

The first couplet, *Ave verum corpus natum de Maria Virgine*—"Hail, true body, truly born / of the Virgin Mary mild"—gives the key to understanding all the rest. Berengarius of Tours denied that the presence of Christ in the sign of bread was real, saying it was only symbolic. In reaction to this heresy, a new emphasis arose, identifying totally the Eucharistic body with the historical body of Christ. All expressions in the first part of the hymn refer to Christ in the flesh: birth from Mary, passion, death, pierced side. The author stops at that point; he makes no mention of the resurrection, lest this should lead one to think of a glorified, spiritual body, not "real" enough.

Theology in our day has developed a more balanced vision of the identity between the historical body of Christ born of Mary and his Eucharistic-body. The tendency now is to rediscover the sacramental character of Christ's presence, which, however real and substantial, is not material. The basic truth affirmed in the hymn, however, remains intact. The very Jesus born of Mary, who "went about doing good" (Acts 10:38), who died on the cross and rose again on the third day, is really present in the world today, not merely in a vague and spiritual way, or as some would say, in the "cause" he stood for. The Eucharist is the way Jesus invented to remain forever Emmanuel, God-with-us.

This presence is a guarantee, not only for the Church, but for the entire world. Yet we feel afraid to use the words "God is with us" because they have been used before in an exclusive sense: God is "with us," on our side, meaning not with others, and even "against" those others who are our enemies. But since Christ has come, there is no longer any exclusiveness; everything has become universal. "God was in Christ reconciling the world to himself, not counting their trespasses against them" (2 Corinthians 5:19)—the whole world, not just a part of it; humankind as a whole, not just one people.

"God is on our side," that is, on the side of humankind, our friend and ally against the powers of evil. God alone personifies the kingdom of good against the kingdom of evil. We need to bear witness to this hope that is in us, rising up against the gloomy wind of pessimism blowing through our society.

24. The God of Love in the Person of Jesus

God's love for people has its roots in eternity—"He chose us . . . before the foundation of the world," says the apostle Paul in Ephesians 1:4—but was manifested in time, in a series of actual gestures that make up the history of salvation. In ancient times, God had frequently spoken to the patriarchs in many and varied ways about this love of his (cf. Hebrews 1:1). He had spoken by creating us, because what is creation if not an act of love, the primordial act of God's love for humanity? Later he spoke through the prophets, because in reality the biblical prophets are nothing other than messengers of God's love, "friends of the Bridegroom." Even their rebukes and threats are intended as a defense of that love of God for his people. In the prophets, God compares his love to that of a mother (cf. Isaiah 49:15), to that of a father (cf. Hosea 11:1-4), to that of a bridegroom (cf. Isaiah 62:5). God himself sums up his whole behavior towards Israel by saying, "I have loved you with an everlasting love" (Jeremiah 31:3)—a phrase unheard of in any philosophy or any religion on the lips of a god! The god of the philosophers is a god to be loved, not a God who loves, and who loves first.

But it was not enough for God to tell us about his love through the prophets. "In these last days he has spoken to us by a Son"

(Hebrews 1:2). There is now an enormous difference, compared to before: Jesus does not confine himself to speaking about God's love, as the prophets did: he *is* the love of God. Because "God is love" (1 John 4:8), and Jesus is God!

25. LONG FOR REPENTANCE

By resurrecting Jesus from the dead, God transformed our greatest sins into his greatest mercy. By killing Jesus, we have killed our sins, which he had taken onto himself. Only if the word "repentance" has reached the bottom of our hearts shall we be able to savor now the floods of light and love enclosed in this joyful Easter message. Whoever has been able to say in all sincerity, "I killed Jesus of Nazareth" knows what it means to be "born anew to a living hope through the resurrection of Jesus Christ from the dead" (1 Peter 1:3). It is like someone being convinced that he has killed another person, who flees in desperation, believing there is no escape in this world for him, when unexpectedly he hears that the person managed to survive and has forgiven him and even wants to be friends with him.

Sin itself holds no fear for us because we no longer bear it by ourselves. He was "raised for our justification" (Romans 4:25), that is, so that he could take our sins and, in exchange, grant us his justice. A repentant man has been "baptized into Jesus' death" (6:3), and now it's as if Jesus were dragging him together with himself out of the tomb and into a new life. "God, who is rich in mercy, out of the great love with which he loved us, even when we were dead through our trespasses, made us alive together with Christ" (Ephesians 2:4-5).

Perhaps you think this joyful message is not for you because your veil hasn't been torn and your eyes haven't overflowed with tears of repentance. Don't be sad and don't despair; this is God's gift, and he can give it to you from one minute to the next or gradually, perhaps when you least expect it. Just persevere untiringly in imploring him and desiring it, just as I do. If you ardently long for repentance, you have already repented! Let yourself be born again to "a living hope," and begin to live your new life.

26. THE FATHER'S DEBT TO THE SON

We have a distorted view of our redemption, and this creates problems of faith for us. We think of it as a sort of bargain: Jesus, the mediator between God and man, pays the Father the price of our ransom with his blood, and the Father is "satisfied" and forgives men their sins. But this is a very human view, inexact or at least partially so. Even humanly speaking, it is unbearable—a father who needs his son's blood to be placated! The truth is that the Son's suffering comes first and foremost (it is spontaneous and free!), and this is so precious in the Father's eyes that he, in return, makes the greatest gift possible to the Son, giving him many brothers, making him "the first-born among many brethren" (Romans 8:29). "Ask of me," he told him, "and I will make the nations your heritage, / and the ends of the earth your possessions" (Psalm 2:8).

Therefore, it is not so much the Son paying a debt to the Father as the Father paying a debt to the Son for having restored to him "all those who had gone astray" (Isaiah 53:6). And he paid it as only God could, in an infinite measure, for none of us could possibly imagine the glory and joy the Father gave Christ in his resurrection.

27. New Life of the Spirit

One day—it was the last day of the feast of Tabernacles—Jesus stood up and exclaimed, "If any man is thirsty, let him come to me! Let the man come and drink who believes in me!" (John 7:37-38, JB). And the Evangelist comments, "He was speaking of the Spirit which those who believed in him were to receive" (7:39, JB). The water, therefore, symbolizes the Spirit. Referring to this episode, St. John's First Letter says, "There are three witnesses, the Spirit, the water and the blood" (5:7-8, JB). These three are not on the same level. The blood and water coming visibly from Christ's side were the signs, the sacraments; the Spirit was the invisible reality hidden in them and acting through them.

Before this moment, the Spirit had not yet come into the world; but now that Jesus had died for us, purifying us from our sins, the Spirit was moving over the face of the waters again as at the beginning of creation (cf. Genesis 1:2). Having exclaimed, "It is accomplished," Jesus "gave up his Spirit" (John 19:30, JB), which means he drew his last breath and died, but also that he gave forth his Spirit, the Holy Spirit! The Evangelist means both. The last breath of Jesus became the first breath of the Church! This was the realization of the work of redemption, its most precious fruit. Redemption was not just the remission of sins; it was also positively the gift of the new life of the Spirit. In fact, this was the aim of the whole thing, and the remission of sins itself is carried out in the Church today only through the Holy Spirit.

28. MARY'S CONSENT

The Second Vatican Council says of Mary at the foot of the cross:

> The Blessed Virgin advanced in her pilgrimage of faith, and faithfully persevered in her union with her Son unto the cross, where she stood, in keeping with the divine plan, grieving exceedingly with her only-begotten Son, uniting herself with a maternal heart with His sacrifice, and lovingly consenting to the immolation of this Victim which she herself had brought forth. (*Lumen Gentium,* 58)

To consent to the immolation of the Victim she herself had brought forth was to immolate herself.

Standing "upright" by the cross, Mary's head was close to her Son's bowed head. Their eyes met. When he said, "Woman, behold, your son!" (John 19:26), Jesus was looking at her and therefore did not need to call her by name to distinguish her from the other women. Who could penetrate the mystery of that look between mother and Son at such a time? A tremendous painful joy passed between them, and their joy sprung from the fact that they were no longer resisting pain; they no longer had any defenses against suffering; they let themselves freely be immersed in it. Peace had taken the place of struggle. They had become one with the suffering and the sin of the whole world— Jesus directly, as "the expiation . . . for the sins of the whole world" (1 John 2:2), and Mary indirectly, through her spiritual and bodily union with her Son.

The last thing Jesus did on the cross before entering the dark moment of his agony and death was to adore the Father's will. Mary was with him in this too. She, too, adored the Father's will before a dreadful solitude and darkness came over her heart just as there was darkness outside over all the land (cf. Matthew 27:45).

And that solitude and adoration remained fixed there, at the center of her life, until her death when the hour of resurrection came for her too.

29. The Peak of Love

Let us . . . make time for the love of Christ to wrap itself around us and enter into us. Let us expose ourselves to this love as to the summer sun. What is the Redeemer's love like?

The first quality is that it is *love for enemies*. "While we were enemies we were reconciled" (Romans 5:10). Jesus had said, "Greater love has no man than this, that a man lay down his life for his friends" (John 15:13). But we must pay attention to what the word "friends" signifies here. John himself shows that there is a still greater love than this, greater than giving one's life for one's *friends;* it is to give it for one's *enemies.* So, then, what does the term "friends" mean here? Not those that love you but those that you love ("friends" has the passive sense of "being loved," not the active sense of "loving"). Jesus called Judas "friend" (cf. Matthew 26:50), not because Judas loved him (he was going to betray him), but because he loved Judas. And what does the word "enemy" signify? Not those you hate but those that hate you ("enemies," on the other hand, has the active sense of "hating" and not the passive sense of "being hated"). God hates no one. He does not consider anyone an enemy. Good and bad, we are all his children.

This is the highest peak, the Everest, of love. We cannot really picture a greater love than this—to die for the enemy, to love those who hate us and wish only to destroy us and are actually destroying us! "Father, forgive them" (Luke 23:34). Father, forgive them! And we were the enemy—we sinners, we the ungodly, we who learned from Adam that dreadful "self-love that, if necessary, drives us to be scornful of God" (Augustine, *On the City of God,* 14, 28). "Surely he has borne our griefs / . . . and the LORD has laid on him / the iniquity of us all . . . / yet he opened not his mouth" (Isaiah 53:4, 6, 7).

O, our Redeemer, how you loved us, how you loved us!

30. BORN OF CHRIST'S DEATH

Christ's cry on the cross was a birth cry, but it was of a singular birth. Some time ago when I was abroad, I heard the sad news that a young wife who was expecting her first baby had a tumor. If she had undergone chemotherapy, the tumor would have been kept under control, but alas, she would almost certainly have lost her baby. A choice had to be made. Her family and public opinion wanted her to save her life, consoling her with the fact that she could have other children. But she was unshakable and refused to be cured. It became a national case and was covered in the press and on television, partly because the topic of abortion was being widely discussed in the country in question at that time. To avoid people's curiosity, the young woman left the town and went back to her parents' home. After a few days, she gave birth to a lovely little girl, and a week later, she herself died.

I wonder what that child will feel when she grows up and hears this? Everything in life will seem like a trifle to her when compared to what her mother did. Sometimes we meet children whose mothers died giving birth to them. They seem different, as if they are protecting a mystery. They seem to know, or want to know, nothing about what happened, but in fact, they listen very carefully to any memory or word spoken about their mother. They distinguish people by how they talk about their mother. Her death is inscribed in their hearts, for they were born out of it.

And so, we are that little girl; we are those children born of a death! "Lord Jesus Christ," the priest says before Communion, "Son of the living God, who by the will of the Father and the work of the Holy Spirit, through your death brought life to the world *(per mortem tuam mundum vivificasti)*." The cry of Jesus on the cross is the cry of one dying while giving life.

31. TRUSTING IN THE FATHER'S LOVE FOR US

A child who is certain of his father's love will grow up strong, secure, happy, and free for life. God's word wants to do this for us; it wants to restore this security to us. Man's solitude in this world cannot be overcome except by faith in God the Father's love. A well-known philosopher wrote that "God's paternal love is the only steadfast thing in life, the real point of Archimedes" (Kierkegaard, *Journals,* III, A73).

Observe a child out walking with his father, holding his father's hand or being swung around by him, and you will have the best picture possible of a happy, free child, full of pride. I read somewhere about a trick that an acrobat once did on the top floor of a skyscraper. He leaned out as far as he could possibly go, supporting himself on the bare tips of his toes and holding his small child in his arms. When he and the child came back down, someone asked the child if he'd been afraid. The child, surprised at the question, answered, "No, I wasn't; my father was holding me!"

God's word wants us to be like that child. After reminding us that God did not spare his own Son for us, St. Paul cries out joyfully and victoriously:

If God is for us, who is against us? . . . Who shall bring any charge against [us]? . . . Who is to condemn? . . . Who shall separate us from the love of Christ? Shall tribulation, or distress, or persecution, or famine, or nakedness, or peril, or sword? . . . No, in all these things we are more than conquerors through him who loved us. (Romans 8:31-37)

And Jesus tells us, therefore, to free ourselves of all fear, of all cowardice, of all discouragement. Your Father knows you, and your Father loves you, Jesus says. You were not given a spirit of slaves to fall back into fear, but a spirit of children to cry out, "*Abba,* Father!" (cf. Romans 8:15-16).

Before such an incomprehensible love, it comes spontaneously to us to turn to Jesus and ask him, "Jesus, you are our elder brother; tell us what we can do to be worthy of so much love and suffering on the Father's part." And from the height of his cross, Jesus answers us not with words but with facts. "There is," he says, "something you can do, something I also did, for it pleases the Father: have confidence in him, trust him against everything, against everyone, against yourselves. When you are in darkness and distress, when difficulties threaten to suffocate you and you are on the point of giving up, pull yourselves together and cry aloud, 'Father, I no longer understand you but I trust you!' And you will find peace again."

32. THE LAST JUDGMENT

People enter the Sistine Chapel in the Vatican and sit and gaze breathlessly at Michelangelo's *Last Judgment*—at the representation, not at the reality being represented! Adulterers, the ambitious, the ungodly, all sit there and exchange comments on the painting. But it does not enter their heads that one of those faces with their eyes full of terror has anything to say to them personally. Michelangelo himself was subjugated by the reality ("Come you blessed. . . . Depart you wicked"), and we are content with his representation.

Much has been said of the restoration of Michelangelo's *Last Judgment*. But there is another last judgment that has to be restored as soon as possible, which is not painted on walls or bricks but in the hearts of Christians. That, too, in fact, has faded and is falling to pieces. "The hereafter (and the last judgment with it) has become a joke, an exigency so uncertain that not only does no one any longer respect it but no one even envisages it, so that people are actually amused at the thought that there used to be a time when this idea transformed everyone's existence" (Kierkegaard, *Concluding Postscript*, II, 4). In some of the old basilicas, the last judgment was depicted on the back walls opposite the altar, behind the congregation and not in front of it. This was so that the people could see it and remember as they emerged from the church into daily life. The idea of the judgment molded their whole existence.

When I was a boy, I saw a scene of a film that I have never forgotten. A railway bridge collapsed over a river in flood. On both sides, sections of the track were hanging in the air. The guard of the nearest level crossing realized what had happened and raced toward the train that was approaching at full speed. It was getting dark, so he ran between the tracks waving a lantern and shouting frantically, "Stop, stop! Go back, go back!"

That train is a vivid representation of us. It is the picture of a society going on carelessly, intoxicated with its conquests and heedless of what lies ahead. The Church must act as the guard did, as it were, and repeat the words Jesus said one day at the news that several people had lost their lives: "Unless you repent you will all likewise perish" (Luke 13:5). Or the words the prophets spoke in their day: "Repent and turn from all your transgressions. . . . Why will you die, O house of Israel?" (Ezekiel 18:30, 31). This could be one of the starting points for a new evangelization.

Someone might try to console himself with the thought that, after all, judgment day is still far off, perhaps millions of years away. Jesus again gives the answer in the gospel: "Fool! This night your soul is required of you" (Luke 12:20). Truly, "the Judge is standing at the doors" (James 5:9). The last breath is hardly drawn before judgment takes place. A flash, and the truth about everything is clear. Theology calls it the "particular judgment," but it is nonetheless final. There can be no revision.

33. LOVING THE POOR

Love the poor: love for Christ and love for the poor are interconnected. Some (like Charles de Foucauld) started by loving Christ and ended up loving the poor. Others (like Simone Weil) started by loving the poor, the ordinary people, and this led them to loving Christ.

To love the poor means, first of all, to respect them and acknowledge their dignity. Precisely because they lack other titles and distinctions, the radical dignity of being human shines more brightly in them.

To love the poor also includes asking their forgiveness: forgiveness for our inability to open our hearts to them with joy; for the distance that, in spite of everything, remains between us; for the continuous humiliations they suffer. Forgiveness for our inert and passive indignation in the face of injustice; for our crude oratory concerning them—each one saying his own bit and thus justifying our own peaceful existence; for our need to know for certain that we are not being tricked before we do the smallest thing for them; for not seeing in them the living tabernacle of the poor and rejected Christ; for not taking their part.

On the other hand, the poor deserve more than just our compassion and commiseration; they deserve our admiration too. They are the real world champions. Every year we witness the assigning of Nobel Prizes, cups, and gold, silver, and bronze medals to the winners of various competitions or in memory of someone's achievements—even, perhaps, simply because some athlete has broken the world record of a two- or four-hundred meters race, or succeeded in jumping a centimeter higher than others, or won a marathon race or a slalom. But if we were to observe the somersaults, the endurance, the slaloms the poor are capable of, and not just once but for a whole lifetime, the performances of the most famous athletes would look like child's play to us.

. . . Love the poor and, finally, *help the poor*. St James said: "If a brother or sister is ill-clad and in lack of daily food, and one of you says to them, 'Go in peace, be warmed and filled,' without giving them the things needed for the body, what does it profit? So faith by itself, if it has no works, is dead" (James 2:15-17). On judgment day, Jesus will not say, "I was naked and you had pity for me," but he will say, "I was naked and you clothed me" (Matthew 25:36).

34. The Devil Has Been Tied

In Christianity, Satan is not someone who holds an importance that is equal but contrary to Christ's. Christianity is not one of the dualistic religions, where God and the devil are taken to be two parallel principles, eternal and independent of each other. According to the Bible, the devil is merely one of God's creatures, but one who has "gone bad"; all that is positive about him comes from God, but he has spoiled it, turning it aside from God's purposes and using it against him. And that said, do we have all the explanation we need? No. The existence of the evil one remains a mystery, like the existence of evil as such, but it is not the only mystery in life.

Neither is it exactly right to say that we believe "in" the devil. We believe "in" God and "in" Jesus Christ, but not "in" the devil, if to believe means to trust someone and to entrust oneself to that person. We believe that there is a devil, but not "in" the devil; he is an *object* and, moreover, a negative object, of our faith, and not at all the one who moves us to believe and who is the *final end* of our faith.

There is no reason to be excessively afraid of the devil. Since Christ came, said one of the ancient authors, the devil has been tied, like a dog on a chain. He cannot bite you, unless of course you pay no heed to the danger and go too close. . . . He can bark, he can entice, but he cannot bite any more unless you want him to. For it is not by compelling us that he can harm us, but only by using persuasion on us; he cannot force our consent, but only solicit it. (Caesarius of Arles, *Sermons*, 121, 6)

To accept what faith teaches about the devil does not diminish human freedom. We need only to take care not to imagine that he is responsible for every fault of ours or for every misfortune that comes upon us. To see the devil around every corner is just as much an aberration as not to see him at all. "The devil is glad when we put the blame on him. In fact, he wants you to blame him. He willingly accepts all your accusations, just as long as that serves to keep you from confessing your sins!" (Augustine, *Sermons*, 20, 2).

35. Redeemed for Eternity

Some polls on religious beliefs have revealed a strange fact: there are, even among believers, some who believe in God but not in a life after death for human beings. Yet how could one think such a thing? The Letter to the Hebrews says that Christ died to win "an eternal redemption" for us (9:12)—redemption not for time only, but eternal. Some object, "But no one has ever come back from the beyond to assure us that it exists in fact and is not merely an illusion." That is not true. There is someone who comes back from beyond death every day to give us that certainty and to renew his promises, if we but know how to listen to him. We are on our way to meet the One who comes to meet us every day in the Eucharist to give us a foretaste (*praegustatum!*) of the eternal banquet of the kingdom.

We need to cry out this, our hope, to help ourselves and others to overcome the horror of death and the mood of gloomy pessimism common in our society. So many reasons are put forward for the desperate state of the world. Scientists research in ever greater detail the possible scenario for the dissolution of the cosmos. The earth and other planets will grow cold, the sun and the stars will cool down, and everything will grow cold. Light will fade; there will be more and more black holes. The universe will be full of gigantic black holes drifting further and further apart until eventually the expansion ceases, the contraction begins, and all matter and all energy collapse into a compact mass of infinite density. It will all end in a grand implosion, the "Big Crunch," and all will return to the emptiness and silence that preceded the Big Bang fifty billion years ago.

No one knows whether things will really go that way or some other way, but faith gives us the assurance that, whatever may happen, it will not be the total and final end. God did not reconcile the world to himself only to abandon it to nothingness; he did not promise to remain with us to the end of the world only to go—alone—back to his heaven when that end comes. "I have loved you with an everlasting love," God says in the Bible (Jeremiah 31:3), and God's promises of "everlasting love" are not like ours.

36. LET EVERY KNEE BOW BEFORE HIM

This evening, when the bare crucifix is lifted up before our eyes, let us gaze upon it. This is the Jesus we proclaim as Lord, not a different one, an easy, rosewater Jesus. What we are about to do is very important. To give us the privilege of calling him "King" and "Lord," as we shall now do, Jesus accepted being called a king in mockery. To give us the privilege of humbly bowing our knee before him, he allowed others to kneel before him in derision. It is written: "[The soldiers] clothed him in a purple cloak, and plaiting a crown of thorns they put it on him. And they began to salute him. . . . And they struck his head with a reed, and spat upon him, and they knelt down in homage to him" (Mark 15:17-18, 19). We must comprehend well what we are doing so as to act in profound adoration and gratitude, for the price he paid is too high for anything less. Alive he only heard "proclamations" of hatred; the "genuflections" he received were ones of ignominy, so let us not add to this with our indifference and superficiality. When he was dying on the cross, he could still hear the deafening echoes of the shouting, and the word "King" hung over his head like a sentence. Now that he is at the right hand of the Father and is present among us in the Spirit, let him see that every knee does in fact bow before him and with it the mind, the heart, the will, and everything. Let him hear this cry of joy bursting from the hearts of the redeemed: "Jesus Christ is Lord, to the glory of God the Father!" (Philippians 2:11).

37. THE SIGNS OF CHRIST'S LOVE

If we want to know how much God loved us, we now have a simple and certain way of knowing: by looking at how much he suffered! Not just in his body, but most of all in his soul, because the true passion of Jesus is the one that cannot be seen, the one that made him cry out in Gethsemane, "My soul is very sorrowful, even to death" (Mark 14:34). Jesus died in his heart before he died physically. Who can fathom the depths of dereliction, sadness, and anguish in Christ's soul as he felt himself "made to be sin" (2 Corinthians 5:21), he who was the innocent Son of the Father? The Good Friday liturgy has rightly placed on Christ's lips the words of Lamentations: "Is it nothing to you, all you who pass by? / Look and see / if there is any sorrow like my sorrow / . . . which the LORD inflicted . . . " (1:12).

It was with this moment in mind that the words *Sic Deus dilexit mundum* were written: "For God so loved the world" (John 3:16). At the beginning of his gospel, John exclaims, "We have beheld his glory" (1:14). If we ask the Evangelist, "Where did you see his glory?" he will reply, "I saw his glory at the foot of the cross!" Because God's glory lies in the fact that he hid his glory for our sake, because he loved us. This is the greatest glory that God has outside of himself, outside of the Trinity, greater even than having created us or having created the entire universe. Seated now at the Father's right hand in glory, Christ's body no longer retains the signs and characteristics of his mortal condition. But the Book of Revelation tells us that there is one thing he does jealously retain and show to the whole court of heaven: his wounds, the signs of his passion (cf. Revelation 5:6). Of these he is proud, because they are the signs of his great love for his creatures.

38. JUSTIFIED THROUGH FAITH

One day, explaining the significance of his death on the cross, Jesus said, "As Moses lifted up the serpent in the wilderness, so must the Son of man be lifted up, that whoever believes in him may have eternal life" (John 3:14-15). To believe is, therefore, the great task we have on Good Friday before the crucified Jesus . He was "raised up" on the cross, and in a mysterious way, he will be there to the end of time (even if he is risen) so that by contemplating him, mankind may believe.

What is it that we must believe? In his Letter to the Romans, St. Paul writes, "But now the righteousness of God has been manifested . . . through faith in Jesus Christ for all who believe. For there is no distinction; since all have sinned and fall short of the glory of God" (Romans 3:21, 22-23). All without distinction—the only distinction being that some are aware of this, some still ignore it, and others have forgotten it. All, therefore, have sinned. But "they are justified by his grace as a gift, through the redemption which is in Jesus Christ, whom God put forward as an expiation by his blood, to be received by faith" (3:24-25).

This is what we must believe: that in Jesus Christ, God offers us the chance to be justified through faith, made righteous as it were, forgiven, saved, made new. This is what "God's righteousness" means. God works his justice by showing mercy.

39. At the Foot of the Cross

S tanding by the cross of Jesus were his mother, and his mother's sister, Mary the wife of Clopas, and Mary Magdalene. When Jesus saw his mother, and the disciple whom he loved standing near, he said to his mother, "Woman, behold, your son!" Then he said to the disciple, "Behold, your mother!" And from that hour the disciple took her to his own home. (John 19:25-27)

These are the words we have just heard during the reading of the passion. And the account of what happened comes to us from John, who was there beneath the cross with Mary. Not much information comes to us from such a direct and sure source as this. And on this Holy Friday, we want to pause and reflect on these words.

If Mary were "standing by the cross of Jesus" on Calvary, it means she was in Jerusalem during those days, and if she was in Jerusalem, it means that she saw all that happened. She was present at the whole of her Son's passion; at the shouting of "Barabbas, Barabbas!" and at the *Ecce homo*! She saw her Son come out scourged and crowned with thorns, covered with spittle; she saw his naked body tremble in the agony of death. She saw the soldiers divide his garments and cast lots for his tunic, which she herself had lovingly woven. She also drank the bitter chalice to the end. The words of desolation of the ancient daughter of Zion are fitting for her: "All you who pass this way, / look and see: / is any sorrow like the sorrow / that afflicts me . . .?" (Lamentations 1:12, JB).

Mary was not alone by the cross. Besides John, there were three other women with her: her sister, Mary, the wife of Clopas, and Mary Magdalene. It might seem that Mary was just one of the many women present. But she was there as "his mother," and that was the difference, as it placed her in a unique position compared with all the others. I have sometimes attended a young person's funeral, and I am now thinking particularly of a young boy's funeral. Several women, all dressed in black and weeping, followed the hearse. They all seemed to be suffering in the same way. But there was one among them who was different. All the others were thinking of her, weeping for her and looking sideways at her. She was the young boy's mother. She stared fixedly at the coffin as if she had turned to stone, and you could see her lips repeating her son's name over and over again. When, at the *Sanctus*, everyone started to repeat with the priest, "Holy, Holy, Holy is the Lord God of the Universe . . . ," she, too, started to murmur mechanically, "Holy, Holy, Holy . . ." At that moment I thought of Mary at the foot of the cross.

But Mary was asked for something much more difficult. She was asked to forgive those who had killed her Son. When she heard her Son saying, "Father, forgive them; for they know not what they do" (Luke 23:34), Mary immediately realized what the heavenly Father wanted from her too, that she should repeat the same words in her heart: "Father, forgive them . . . " And she repeated them. She forgave.

40. The Holy Spirit among Us

Someone could say, "Yes, it's true that Jesus once loved us when he was on earth, but now? Now that he is no longer among us, what is left of that love of his, except for a faint memory?" The disciples of Emmaus said, "Three days have already gone by," and we are tempted to say, "Two thousand years have already gone by!" But they were wrong, because Jesus was risen and was walking by their side, just as we are wrong when we think like them. In fact, his love is still among us because "God's love has been poured into our hearts through the Holy Spirit who has been given to us" (Romans 5:5).

And here is the second great truth we celebrate today, no less beautiful and important than the first: God loved the world so much that he gave us the Holy Spirit! The water flowing from Christ's side, together with the blood, was the symbol of the Holy Spirit. "By this we know that we abide in him and he in us, because he has given us of his own Spirit" (1 John 4:13). Let us remember this phrase of John's—it sums up everything. It means that Jesus has left us as a gift his whole self, his whole love, because "in the spirit he was raised to life" (1 Peter 3:18-19, JB).

41. Have the Mind of Christ

Jesus tells us in the gospel, "Learn from me; for I am gentle and lowly in heart" (Matthew 11:29). And what did Jesus ever do to call himself humble? Did he think lowly or talk lowly of himself? On the contrary, he proclaimed himself "Master and Lord," one who is greater than Jonah, than Solomon, than Abraham, than everyone. What, then, did he do? He took "the form of a servant" (Philippians 2:7). He did not *consider* himself small, nor did he *proclaim* himself small, but he *made* himself small to serve us. He made himself "last of all and servant of all" (Mark 9:35). Christ was not afraid to compromise his divine dignity when he humbled himself to become a man like other men.

Christ's humility is made up of obedience as well as service: "He humbled himself and became obedient unto death" (Philippians 2:8). Humility and obedience appear to be almost the same thing here. Jesus on the cross is humble because he offers no resistance to the Father's will. . . .

On the cross, Jesus did not just reveal or practice humility; he created it too. True Christian humility now consists in participating in Christ's inner state on the cross. The apostle Paul says, "Have this mind among yourselves, which was in Christ Jesus" (Philippians 2:5)—the same mind and not a similar one.

42. For Each of Us!

The Redeemer's love is *a personal love*. Christ died "for us," St. Paul told us. If we understand the "for us" only in a collective sense, we deprive it of some of its greatness. The numeric disproportion reestablishes a certain proportion of value. It is true that Jesus is innocent and we are guilty, that he is God and we are men; but after all, he is just one and we are billions. It might seem more plausible that one should die to save the lives of billions. But this is not the case. He died "for us" means also "for each one of us." It must be taken in a distributive sense as well as in a collective sense. As St. Paul says, "[He] loved *me* and gave himself for *me*" (Galatians 2:20, emphasis added).

Therefore, Christ did not love the masses but individuals, persons. He died also for me, and I must conclude that he would have died just the same even if I had been the only one on the face of the earth to save. This is a certainty of faith. Christ's love is infinite because it is divine and not only human. (Christ is also God, and we must never, even for an instant, forget this!) But the infinite cannot split into parts. It is all in all. Millions of particles are consecrated every day in churches. But each of these does not contain only a particle of Christ's body but the whole Christ. It is the same with his love. There are billions of people, and each one does not receive only a particle of Christ's love but the fullness of his love, whole and entire. All of Christ's love is in me and also in my neighbor, and this fact should make me respect him and have regard and charity for him.

I, too, can say, "Christ loved me and gave his life for me!" He knows his sheep by name, and he calls them by name (cf. John 10:3). No one is just a number for him. How new and true do God's words, through Isaiah the prophet, ring on the lips of Jesus on the cross: "Fear not, for I have redeemed you; / I have called you by name, you are mine. /. . . Because you are precious in my eyes, / and honored, and I love you" (43:1, 4). You are honored because I love you: it is all expressed in the singular tense here. How sweet these words would sound to those who feel miserable, worthless, abandoned by all, if only they were courageous enough to believe them!

"Who shall separate us from the love of Christ?" St. Paul exclaims. "Shall tribulation, or distress . . . ?" (Romans 8:35). No, nothing will be able to separate us (cf. 8:37-39). This discovery can change a man's life; this is the news that we must never tire of shouting out to people today. This is the only sure and steady fact in this world: that God loves us!

43. A Sword Hangs over Us

A Greek historian recounts how one day Damocles wanted to show an envious subject how a king lives. He invited this man to a lavish dinner, and life at court seemed even more enviable to him. At a certain point, the king asked him to raise his eyes, and the man realized that he was sitting directly beneath a sword dangling from a single hair! He was terrified, almost choked, and began to tremble. "This," Damocles told him, "is how kings live, with a sword poised above them day and night."

This is not only true of kings. A sword of Damocles hangs over the head of every person, without exception. Yet people, intent as they are on their own affairs and distractions, pay no heed. The name of this sword is death. And it is out of love for mankind, not hatred, that from time to time the Church must perform the thankless task of inviting us to raise our eyes and see this sword poised above us, so that when it falls, we shall be ready for it.

But are we not already tormented enough by the thought of death? What need is there to sink the knife deeper into the wound? This is very true. The fear of death is ingrained in every human being. A well-known psychologist said that the death angst is "the worm at the core of each thought." It is the spontaneous expression of the strongest of all human instincts: the instinct for self-preservation. If we could hear the silent cry that torments mankind, we would hear this horrifying scream: "I do not want to die!"

Why, then, should man be invited to reflect on death if he is so aware of it? The reason is that we have simply chosen to remove it. We pretend it does not exist, or at least that it only affects other people. After the war, a new luxury residential area was built in one of Italy's big cities. The builders decided not to build a church there so that the residents would never be disturbed by the sound of a death bell or the sight of a funeral.

But the thought of death cannot be so easily removed or put aside. All we can do is repress it, which is what most of us do, and repressing something is a hard job; it requires constant attention and psychological effort. It is like trying to press down a lid on something that keeps bubbling up. We expend a lot of energy trying to keep the thought of death at bay. Some people pretend not to be frightened by death at all. They say they know they must die, but this thought does not particularly disturb them; they prefer to think of life rather than of death. But this is secularized posturing; in actual fact, it is simply one of the many ways of repressing the fear of death.

That is why it is time to have a good talk about death, and what better time is there than Good Friday, the day on which it was defeated? We do this, not to increase our fear of death, but to be freed from it, by the only One who is able to do this.

44. CROSSING OVER

Before he died, Jesus instituted the Eucharist, and in doing so, anticipated his own death. He showed that his death was not just a chance occurrence or the result of human decisions. He gave it significance, the significance he—not his enemies—intended it to have. He made it a memorial of the new covenant, an expiation of sin, the supreme gift of love to the Father for all men. "Take this," he said, "and eat; this is my body given for you" (cf. Luke 22:19).

At every Mass we, too, are given this wonderful opportunity of giving meaning to our death before it actually takes place, of uniting ourselves to Christ so as to make it a living sacrifice to him, a libation to be poured away, as St. Paul says (cf. 2 Timothy 4:6).

One day by the lakeside, with the coming of evening, Jesus said to his disciples, "Let us cross over to the other side" (Mark 4:35). The day or the evening will come when he will say those same words to us too: "Let us cross over to the other side." Blessed are those who, like the disciples, are ready to take him "just as he was" (4:36), and set sail with him in faith.

Today a profound thank you explodes from the hearts of believers and from the whole of mankind: thank you, Lord Jesus Christ, in the name of those who know you died for them, and of those who do not know. Thank you for sweating blood for us, for your distress, and for your cry of victory from the cross. Embrace those now departing this world, and repeat to them what you said to the good thief on the cross: "Today you will be with me in Paradise" (Luke 23:43). Stay with us, Lord, for it is evening, and life is declining. . . .

45. God's Unbelievable Love for Us!

D o we really believe that God loves us? No, we don't really believe it, or at least not strongly enough! And if we were to believe it, everything—our lives, ourselves, things, and events—would be transfigured before our eyes. This very day we would be in paradise with him, for paradise is simply rejoicing in God's love. An extracanonical saying attributed to Jesus says, "Whoever is amazed will reign." And this is the realization of these words. Whoever before God's unbelievable love for us is seized with a profound sense of awe, whoever remains speechless before this love, will immediately enter the kingdom of heaven!

But, as I have said, we really don't believe that God loves us; it is ever more difficult to believe in love in this world. There is too much unfaithfulness, too many disappointments. Anyone who has been betrayed or hurt once is afraid to love again and be loved, because he knows how much pain another betrayal would mean. And so the numbers of those unable to believe in God's love or, rather, in any love, go on increasing. The world and life are falling back into an Ice Age. The earth remains, as Dante says, "that flowerbed which makes us so ferocious" (*Paradiso,* XXII, 151).

Then on a personal level, our own unworthiness tempts us: "It is true that God's love is a beautiful thing, but it's not for me! How could God love anyone as unfaithful and negligent as I am? I am not worthy." But let us listen to what God says to us: "Whenever our hearts condemn us, God is greater than our hearts" (cf. 1 John 3:20).

46. "It Is Accomplished"

After Jesus had taken the vinegar he said, 'It is accomplished'; and bowing his head he gave up his spirit" (John 19:30, JB).

"It is accomplished!" This word is enough to throw light on the whole of the mystery of Calvary. What was it that was accomplished? First of all, it was the earthly life of Jesus, the work that the Father had given him to do (cf. John 4:34; 5:36; 17:4). "He had always loved those who were his in the world, but now he showed how perfect his love was" (John 13:1, JB). The Greek says, "He loved them to the *telos*," that is, to the end, and that same word, in its verbal form, is echoed in the cry of Jesus: "*tetelestai*," it is accomplished. He has endured, to the very end, the supreme test of his love.

The Scriptures, too, were accomplished—the Scriptures of the suffering servant, the paschal lamb, the innocent pierced, Ezekiel's vision of the new temple and the river of living water flowing from its side (cf. 47:1-12). But it was not only some particular points of the Scriptures that were accomplished; the entire Old Testament, *en bloc*, had been accomplished, not analytically, but in synthesis, substantively. Dying, the Lamb opened the book with seven seals (cf. Revelation 5:1–8:1) and revealed the full meaning of God's plan.

This is the page that, when you turn it, explains all, like that great illuminated page in the Missal at the beginning of the Canon. See it there, printed in flaming red, the great page that separates the two Testaments. All doors open at once, all points of opposition disappear, all contradictions are resolved. (Paul Claudel, *Le poète et la Bible*, 729)

The page that *separates* the two Testaments is also the page that *joins them together*; each throws light on the other. Nothing is done away with; all is accomplished, fulfilled.

In bringing things to their fulfilment, Christ overcomes their limitations; he makes them take a qualitative leap. It is like what happens in the consecration of the Eucharist: from that moment on, the bread is no longer merely bread; it has become something else. So, too, the old covenant, from the moment of the death of Christ, has become the new and eternal covenant; the letter has become Spirit.

Into the Old comes the New,
into law comes grace,
into the figure, the reality,
into the lamb, the Son,
and into man, God. (Melito of Sardis, *On Easter*, 7)

47. THE CROSS OF LOVE

Yes, God is love! It has been said that if all the Bibles of the world were to be destroyed by some cataclysm or iconoclastic rage, and only one copy remained; and if this copy was also so damaged that only one page was still whole; and likewise if this page was so wrinkled that only one line could still be read—if that line were the line of the First Letter of John where it is written that "God is love," then the whole Bible would have been saved, because the whole content is there.

I lived my childhood in a cottage only a few meters from a high-tension electrical wire, but we lived in darkness or with the light of candles. Between us and the electrical wire was a railway, and with the war going on, nobody thought of overcoming the small obstacle. This is what happens with the love of God: it is there, within our grasp, capable of illuminating and warming everything in our life, but we live out our existence in darkness and cold. This is the only true reason for sadness in life.

God is love, and the cross of Christ is the supreme proof, the historical demonstration. There are two ways of manifesting one's love toward someone, said Nicholas Cabasilas, an Eastern Byzantine author. The first consists of doing good to the person loved, of giving gifts; the second, much more demanding, consists of suffering for him. God has loved us in the first way, that is, with a munificent love, in creation, when he filled us with gifts within and outside of us. He has loved us with a suffering love in the redemption, when he invented his own annihilation, suffering for us the most terrible torments, for the purpose of convincing us of his love. Therefore, it is on the cross that one must now contemplate the truth that "God is love."

48. They Believe in Love!

The world needs to believe in God's love. We must therefore start again to proclaim the gospel of God's love in Jesus Christ. If we don't do so, we shall be like men who place their candles under a bushel basket (cf. Matthew 5:15; Mark 4:21; Luke 11:33). We shall be defrauding the world of its most secret expectation. There are others in the world besides Christians who preach about social justice and respect for man; but there is no one, and I repeat no one, among philosophers or other religions that tells man that God loves him, and loved him first. Yet it is this truth that sustains everything; it is the motive power behind everything. Even the cause of the poor and oppressed is a lost cause in itself if it isn't based on the unshakable truth that God loves us, and he loves the poor and the oppressed.

However, words and bewailings are not enough. Like Jesus, we must be ready to suffer and forgive those who cause suffering. "Father, forgive them" (Luke 23:34)—Jesus uttered these words on the cross, and he left them to us Christians so that we would keep them alive throughout the centuries and arm ourselves with them. And these words were intended, not simply to forgive the enemies Jesus had at that time and who are no longer alive, but to forgive his enemies today, our enemies, the enemies of the Church. Christianity is the religion of forgiving enemies! Only when God's love has helped a man to forgive an enemy at least once can he claim to know God's love that was poured into his heart by the Holy Spirit (cf. Romans 5:5). We should publicly thank those brothers in faith who, when touched by hatred or violent murder, humbly followed the impulse of the Holy Spirit to forgive, even publicly, those who had murdered their dear ones. They believe in love! They have been splendid witnesses in showing that Christ's love, manifested to us on the cross today, is still possible in the Spirit, and that only this love can bring about a change in the world, because it changes hearts.

49. THE SEAMLESS TUNIC AND THE UNITY OF THE CHURCH

The unity of the Church," St. Cyprian writes, "is expressed in the Gospel when it is said that the tunic of Christ was not divided or cut." The glad tidings to proclaim on Good Friday are that unity, before it is a goal to be sought, is a gift to be received. That the tunic is woven "from the top down," St. Cyprian continues, means that "the unity brought by Christ comes from above, from the heavenly Father, and because of this it cannot be broken apart by those who receive it, but must be received in its integrity" (*De unitate Ecclesiae*, 7; cf. John 19:23-24).

The soldiers divided "the clothes" or the "the cloak" (*ta imatia*) into four pieces, that is, Jesus' outer garments, not the tunic, the *chiton*, the inner garment, which was in direct contact with his body. This is also a symbol. We men can divide the human and visible element of the Church, but not its deeper unity, which is identified with the Holy Spirit. Christ's tunic was not and can never be divided. It, too, is of a single piece. "Can Christ be divided?" Paul cried out (cf. 1 Corinthians 1:13). It is the faith that we profess in the Creed: I believe in the Church, one, holy, catholic, and apostolic.

But if unity must serve as a sign "so that the world may believe" (John 17:21), it must also be a visible, communitarian unity. This is the unity that has been lost and must be rediscovered. It is much more than maintaining neighborly relations; it is the mystical interior unity itself—"one body and one Spirit, . . . one hope . . . , one Lord, one faith, one baptism, one God and Father of us all" (Ephesians 4:4-6)—insofar as this objective unity is in fact received, lived, and manifested by believers. It is a unity that is not endangered by diversity, but enriched by it.

After Easter the apostles asked Jesus, "Lord, will you at this time restore the kingdom to Israel?" (Acts 1:6). Today we often address the same question to God: "Is this the time in which you will restore the visible unity of the Church?" God's answer is also the same as the one Jesus gave to the disciples: "It is not for you to know the times or seasons that the Father has fixed by his own authority. But you shall receive power when the Holy Spirit comes upon you; and you shall be my witnesses" (Acts 1:7-8). . . . Today, as well, the Holy Spirit will be the one to lead us into unity, if we let him guide us. . . .

For a century now, we have seen the same thing that happened at Pentecost repeat itself before our eyes on a global scale. God has poured out the Holy Spirit in a new and unusual way upon millions of believers from every Christian denomination, and so that there would be no doubts about his intentions, he poured out the Spirit with the same manifestations. Is this not a sign that the Spirit moves us to recognize each other as disciples of Christ and work toward unity?

50. THE COSMIC SIGNIFICANCE OF THE CROSS

In Paul's eyes, the cross assumes a cosmic significance. Christ has torn down the wall of separation with it; he has reconciled men with God and with each other, destroying hatred (cf. Ephesians 2:14-16). Based on this truth, primitive tradition developed the theme of the cross as a cosmic tree that joins heaven and earth with the vertical branch and unites the different peoples of the world with the horizontal branch. It is both a cosmic and a very personal event at the same time: "[He] loved me and gave himself for me!" (Galatians 2:20); every man, as the apostle writes, is "one for whom Christ died" (Romans 14:15).

From all of this arises the sense of the cross, no longer as a punishment, admonishment, or reason for affliction, but, rather, a glory and the boast of a Christian—that is, a joyful security accompanied by heartfelt gratitude, to which man rises in faith: "But as for me, it is out of the question that I should boast at all, except of the cross of our Lord Jesus Christ" (Galatians 6:14, NJB).

Paul has planted the cross at the center of the Church like the mainmast at the center of the ship. He has made it the foundation and the center of gravity of everything. He has established the permanent framework of the Christian message. The gospels, written after him, follow his framework, making the story

of Christ's passion and death the fulcrum toward which everything is oriented.

51. THE CROSS IS GOD'S YES TO THE WORLD

In his passion, writes St. Paul to Timothy, Jesus Christ "has witnessed to his noble profession of faith " (1 Timothy 6:13, NJB). We ask ourselves: witness to what? Not of the truth of his life or the rightness of his cause. Many have died, and still die today, for a wrong cause, while believing it to be right. Now, the resurrection certainly does testify to the truth of Christ. "God has publicly proved this by raising [Jesus] from the dead," as the apostle Paul was to say in the Areopagus at Athens (Acts 17:31, NJB).

Death testifies not to the truth of Christ but to his love. Of that love, in fact, it is the supreme proof. "No one can have greater love than to lay down his life for his friends" (John 15:13, NJB). One could object that there is a greater love than giving your life for your friends, and that is to give your life for your enemies. But that is precisely what Jesus has done: "Christ died for the godless," writes St. Paul in the Letter to the Romans. "You could hardly find anyone ready to die even for someone upright; though it is just possible that, for a really good person, someone might undertake to die. So it is proof of God's own love for us, that Christ died for us while we were still sinners" (Romans 5:6-8, NJB). "He loved us while we were enemies, so that he could turn us into friends," exclaims St. Augustine (*Commentary on the First Letter of John*, 9, 9; PL 35:2051).

A certain one-sided "theology of the cross" can make us forget the essential point. The cross is not only God's judgment on the world and its wisdom; it is more than the revelation and condemnation of sin. It is not God's NO to the world; it is the YES God speaks to the world from the depths of his love. "That which is wrong," writes Pope Benedict XVI in his book about Jesus,

> the reality of evil, cannot simply be ignored; it cannot just be left to stand. It must be dealt with; it must be overcome. Only this counts as true mercy. And the fact that God now confronts evil himself, because men are incapable of doing so—therein lies the "unconditional" goodness of God. (*Jesus of Nazareth: Holy Week: From the Entrance Into Jerusalem to the Resurrection, Volume 2,* 133)

52. THE CONFESSION OF THE GOOD THIEF

The good thief made a complete confession of sin. He says to his companion who insults Jesus, "Do you not fear God, since you are under the same sentence of condemnation? And we indeed justly; for we are receiving the due reward of our deeds; but this man has done nothing wrong" (Luke 23:40-41). Here the good thief shows himself an excellent theologian. Only God, in fact, if he suffers, suffers absolutely as innocent; every other being who suffers should say, "I suffer justly," because even if he is not responsible for the action imputed to him, he is never altogether without fault. Only the pain of innocent children is similar to God's, and because of this, it is so mysterious and so sacred.

How many atrocious crimes in recent times remain anonymous; how many unresolved cases exist! The good thief launches an appeal to those responsible: "Do like me; come out into the open, confess your fault. You also will experience the joy I had when I heard Jesus' word, 'Today you will be with me in Paradise!'" (Luke 23:43). How many confessed offenders can confirm that it was also like this for them—that they passed from hell to heaven the day they had the courage to repent and confess their fault? I have known some myself. The paradise promised is peace of conscience, the possibility of looking at oneself in the mirror or of looking at one's children without having to have contempt for oneself.

53. The Crown of Victory Is Ours!

Some ancient Fathers of the Church encapsulated in an image the whole mystery of the redemption. Imagine, they said, that an epic fight took place in the stadium. A courageous man confronted a cruel tyrant who had enslaved the city and, with enormous effort and suffering, the man defeated him. You were on the terraces; you did not fight or make an effort or get wounded. However, if you admire the courageous man; if you rejoice with him over his victory; if you intertwine crowns, arouse and stir the assembly for him; if you kneel joyfully before the triumphant one, kiss his head, and shake his right hand—in a word, if you rave so much as to consider his victory yours—I tell you that you will certainly have part of the victor's prize.

However, there is more: imagine that the victor had himself no need of the prize he had won, but wishes more than anything to see his supporter honored and considers as the prize of his combat the crowning of his friend. In that case, perhaps, will that man not obtain the crown also, though he has not toiled or been wounded? He certainly will obtain it! (Nicholas Cabasilas, *Vita in Christo*, I.9; PG 150:517).

It happens thus, say the Fathers, between Christ and us. On the cross he defeated the ancient enemy. "Our swords," exclaims St. John Chrysostom, were not bloodied; we were not in agony; we were not wounded; we did not even see the battle; and yet we obtain the victory. His was the fight, ours the crown. And because we are also the conquerors, let us imitate what soldiers do in such cases: with joyful voices let us exalt the victory, let us intone hymns of praise to the Lord! (*De coemeterio et de cruce*, PG 49:596)

It is not possible to explain better the meaning of the liturgy we are celebrating.

54. Reasons of the Heart

We have always asked how it was that the pious women were the first to see the Risen One and to be given the task of taking the news to the apostles. This was the surest way to make the resurrection hardly credible at all. The testimony of a woman carried no weight whatsoever in a judgment. Perhaps for this very reason, no woman is mentioned in Paul's long list of those who had seen the risen Christ (cf. 1 Corinthians 15:5-8). The apostles themselves at first took the women's words as pure womanly "nonsense" (Luke 24:11, JB)—and gave them no credence.

Authors of antiquity thought they knew the answer to the question. The women, said Romanos Melodos, were the first to see Christ risen because a woman, Eve, was the first to sin! But the true answer is quite different: the women were the first to see Jesus risen because they were the last to leave him in his death, and even when he was dead, they came to bring spices to the tomb (cf. Mark 16:1).

We need to ask ourselves why this was so: why did these women remain firm despite the scandal of the cross? Why did they remain close when all seemed to be over, and even those who had been his most intimate disciples had abandoned Jesus and were getting ready to go home again?

It was Jesus himself who gave us the answer, in anticipation, when he replied to Simon that the sinner who had bathed and kissed his feet had "shown such great love" (Luke 7:47, JB). The women followed Jesus for his own sake, out of gratitude for the good they had received from him, and not for any hope of making a career out of following him. No promise of "twelve thrones" was made to them (cf. Luke 22:28-30), nor did any of them ask for seats on his right and his left in his kingdom (cf. Matthew 20:20-22). They followed, it is written, "to look after him" (Matthew 27:56, JB) and "to provide for them out of their own resources" (Luke 8:3, JB). They were the only ones, after Mary, his mother, that truly made the spirit of the gospel their own. They followed for reasons of the heart, and these did not deceive them.

55. He Is Risen!

How grateful we ought to be to the pious women! On the way of the cross, their sobbing was the only friendly sound to reach the ears of the Savior; while he hung on the cross, their eyes were the only ones to rest on him with compassion and love. . . .

It was not only the part they played in the passion but also the part they played in the resurrection that makes the pious women an example for all Christians today. Throughout the Bible, in chapter after chapter, we read the imperative "Go!" spoken by God to those whom he sends. The word was spoken to Abraham, to Moses: "Go down, Moses, way down in Egypt's land!" (cf. Exodus 3:7); to the prophets; to the apostles: "Go out to the whole world; proclaim the Good News to all creation" (Mark 16:16, JB).

Yet all of these calls were addressed to men. There is only one "Go!" spoken to women: the one Jesus spoke to these women as they brought perfume to anoint him on Easter morning: "Then Jesus said to them, 'Do not be afraid; go and tell my brothers that they must leave for Galilee; they will see me there'" (Matthew 28:10, JB). By these words, he appointed them the first witnesses to the resurrection, "teachers of the teachers" as one of the ancient writers, Gregory of Antioch, has called them.

It is a great pity that because she has been mistakenly identified as the sinful woman who washed the feet of Jesus (cf. Luke 7:37), Mary Magdalene has ended up as fuel for an endless array of legends, ancient and modern, and has been taken up in art and piety almost exclusively as "the penitent" rather than in her primary role as witness to the resurrection (cf. John 20:16-18), "apostle to the apostles," as St. Thomas Aquinas called her.

"Filled with awe and great joy the women came quickly away from the tomb and ran to tell the disciples" (Matthew 28:8, JB). Christian women, all of you, keep on talking to the successors of the apostles, to us priests who are their helpers, telling them the joyful news: "The Master is alive! He is risen! He goes before you to Galilee" (cf. Mark 16:6-8)—which is to say, "He goes before you wherever you go! Do not be afraid!"

Keep alive the sublime exchange between the Church and Mary Magdalene in the Sequence for Easter: "Death with life contended: / combat strangely ended! / Life's own Champion, / slain, yet lives to reign." Life has triumphed over death: it happened for Christ, and it will happen one day for us too.

the WORD among us ®

The *Spirit* of Catholic Living

This book was published by The Word Among Us. For more than thirty years, The Word Among Us has been answering the call of the Second Vatican Council to help Catholic laypeople encounter Christ in the Scriptures—a call reiterated by Pope Benedict XVI and a Synod of Bishops.

The name of our company comes from the prologue to the Gospel of John and reflects the vision and purpose of all of our publications: to be an instrument of the Spirit, whose desire is to manifest Jesus' presence in and to the children of God. In this way we hope to contribute to the Church's ongoing mission of proclaiming the gospel to the world and growing ever more deeply in our love for the Lord.

Our monthly devotional magazine, *The Word Among Us*, features meditations on the daily and Sunday Mass readings, and currently reaches more than one million Catholics in North America each year and another 500,000 Catholics in 100 countries. Our press division has published nearly 200 books and Bible studies over the past 12 years.

To learn more about who we are and what we publish, log on to our website at **www.wau.org**. There you will find a variety of Catholic resources that will help you grow in your faith.

Embrace His Word, Listen to God . . .